Imperfect Perfections

A Random Collection

Kristen Christensen

BookLeaf
Publishing

India | USA | UK

Made with ❤ on the BookLeaf Publishing Platform

www.bookleafpub.in

www.bookleafpub.com

Dedication

To my children...may you always shoot for the moon.

Preface

Poetry is something that has helped me on my healing journey. Hopefully some of what I have written will help you as well.

Acknowledgements

Bookleaf Publishing, I am so very grateful for the writing challenges you offer! This has been such a great opportunity for me!

To Celeste Alder and Amy Brinkerhoff, thank you for being there and supporting me.

1. Shang

Let's take a minute and think about Shang. The horror that he had to have felt when he realized he wanted to bang Ping. In that day and age, it was unheard of and absurd. Shang was this badass warrior, who was determined to build these "boys" into "men". He started by being annoyed and didn't want to be around them more than necessary. Ping shows resilience and determination and Shang starts to hang out with him. One day while writing his missive for the day, Shang finds his mind wandering to Ping. Wondering what his lips might taste like, what his body looks like now that the lean muscle is building. Mentally slapping himself out of those weird and forbidden thoughts, Shang goes and talks to his advisor. The advisor informs him that Shang is not doing as well as he thought he was. Feeling humiliated Shang rushes from the tent only to find that Ping was standing outside and heard the whole thing. Flushing with embarrassment Shang goes to rush by when Ping states, "For what it's worth I think you are a great captain." As Shang walks away he feels Ping's gaze on him and thinks, "Am I crazy? Was he flirting with me?". Days go by and Ping fights valiantly against the Huns, unfortunately, he is hurt. Shang feels a sense of dread and panic, "How can I go on without telling him how I feel? How can I tell him I feel this way? I can't...I have to keep it to myself. He can't die yet, he has barely lived." The doctor leaves the tent and shakes his head at Shang. Shang feels a pang of unease and follows the doctor. The doctor informs him that Ping is not a he but a she. Shang is relieved, betrayed, overjoyed, and hurt all at once. He isn't going crazy, he doesn't have to worry about judgment, he can openly like Ping now. Why did Ping lie? Why would a woman join the army? With so many questions tumbling in his mind, Shang goes inside the tent. There sits Ping with just a small sheet covering his...I mean her body. Ping smiles when he sees Shang and Shang's heart flutters. "Who are you and why are you in my army?" Shang asks the hurt deepening in his voice. "Mulan," came the small reply, "My father was hurt and I didn't want him to die so I took his place." A measure of respect grows within, but Shang thinks, "Now is my chance at my happily ever after." You know how the story ends, they fight, they grow, and Shang and Ping-ahem-Mulan live happily ever after.

2. Winter

Few things about winter bring any joy
Things like reading, hot chocolate, and blankets
Make winter great, snowmen, and celebrate a little boy.
My ultimate favorite is Christmas with its little trinkets.

Dark and dreary it really gets old
The hustle and bustle of the endless shopping
When you are constantly shivering from the cold.
My favorite thing to do is go home bopping
Heated blankets, fuzzy socks, hoodies, and sweats, are
gold.

3. Friends

Friends are people who cheer you on
Who wants the best for you no matter what
They are the ones who lift you up,
Meet you in your mess, see you at your best,
And see you at your worst, and love you
No matter what.

4. Man's Best Friend

Licking your face and causing laughter
Dogs are such a health benefactor
They guard you, love you, and make life complete.
Their company is some you just can't beat.

5. Lenient

Ladies and gentlemen, mothers and fathers
Entangled in the thick of life, are trying to be
Nice to their kids and often tend to
Interpret their children's thoughts and
Emotions. Try to help them
Navigate through those emotions by
Talking things through and being understanding.

6. Coping Mechanism

Beauty and the Beast is my favorite Disney movie
Pocahontas and Sleeping Beauty are also quite groovy.
When needing comfort I turn on one of these shows
And cover myself in a blanket and wallow in my woes.
It's interesting the things that pull you from a mental
floozie.

When needing an escape from reality,
I turn to the books with a sense of finality.
I can lose myself within the pages and feel free
Help me to feel a little less like a banshee.
So I can focus on what's next without a sense of
brutality.

Drawing and coloring can also be cathartic
Sometimes when life is tough and I'm lethargic
Drawing or coloring is what calms and steadies me
I'm not an artist but that doesn't stop my tick
Of trying to tame the energy that begs to be set free.

7. Reading

Grab a book and read
The words flint about the page
Dying to be read

The story grows bold
slowly unfurling intrigue
You grip the pages

Ensue happy sighs
Your eyes dart about frantic
Eager to drink in

Each little detail
You have to absorb it all
Through each page, you fall

Until you are lost
In the world of make-believe

Content to hide there

8. Bad Day

You left me today. You decided that I wasn't worth
fighting for.
I didn't want to be in a relationship, you chased me,
convinced me you wanted me.
I let my guard down and let you in, I didn't know it'd
end with my roar.
The cry of pain that left me once you shut the door. I
silently scream a plea,
That I will survive this hole in my chest, at least to some
degree.
I can't fathom why you'd leave when I have two of your
babies in my tummy.
These little babies have been moving around, making
themselves known causing glee.
I thought you were happy too, I thought maybe I had
finally found my honey.
I hoped you were different, you seemed to be, but I guess
I'm just not that lucky.
For months once the kids were in bed I would cry out in
agony,

Just hoping for the day that I would again feel like my
life was more than mucky.
You leaving wasn't just a bad day for me. It was a day
that brought tragedy.
You finally came to your senses and asked for
forgiveness, but I was wary,
I didn't know if you could be trusted. Eventually, you
convinced me to marry.
At first, it was hard to believe one another, but we
worked and worked.
Sometimes we didn't know if we'd survive because
things got hairy.
Through it all we worked together, we never shirked.
You are the best thing that has ever happened to me no
matter the rocky start.
Man of mine, you have my heart.

9. Grotesque Image

Skin pale and slightly blue, why is he such a weird hue?
Hunched over, I get close, I gasp, and then inhale.
Lips a bluish purple, blood caked on them, did he
struggle?
He looked as if he was just asleep, but was he in pain?
Did it hurt him to die? I cry helplessly in the shower as I
wonder why.
Why did he have to be alone? Why didn't I call sooner?
Could I have
done something, like save his life? "You were the last one
he tried to
Contact," the EMTs implied that he knew he was dying
and wanted
me to know. I raged and cried and broke in two. My Dad
was my Dad
Through and through. Since that hard day in 2019, I've
come to the
realization that life doesn't always work out the way you
want it to.
I love my Dad and I know for a fact that his time was up.

He's in a better
Place now and watches over me.

10. Invisible

Shaking silently no one notices as my hand roams to my neck. Gripping a piece of the soft flesh, I tug it between my finger and thumb. Feeling the soft, smooth skin my thoughts roam freely. As my mind wanders through the many different paths. I notice my neck is sore and force my fingers to cease their restless stirrings. Lowering my hand to my thigh, I become aware of my erratic breathing and force a deep sigh. Oh to be the one who is finally noticed for once. It gets old struggling silently and bearing the weight of the world alone. I'm fine I say in a chipper tone. I'm not and I recognize when others claim to be fine but really aren't. Why can't anyone see my silent plea? I don't always want to be the strong one, sometimes I want to break down and cry. But instead, I sit invisibly by and just wait for the feeling to subside.

11. Nightmare

I had a bad nightmare.

I went to court once again to fight against the awful man.

Once I left court I saw a missed call from my Dad.

"I'll call him in a while," I thought, "I know he won't feel bad."

After an hour or two I tried to call him back, and straight to voicemail it went.

A little later, I tried again, but still no luck, so I shot him a text.

A sense of dread soon began to build, anxiety roiled in its wake.

Again, and again, I tried. Still, he didn't answer or reply.

With a sense of determination, I called my brother to see
if he had heard from him.

He had not, so I called my other brother to check on
him.

No one answered the door, no one seemed to be home he
said.

My brother sent his girlfriend to check. She called me
saying he was unresponsive.

I loaded my kids into the car and to Hinckley I flew. I
gave my kids my phone and in I ran.

Up the stairs heart pounding, mouth dry, sort of feeling
like I could cry.

Macy sat on the top stair, weeping silently as I moved
past stirring her hair.

I ran in and there he sat, hunched over as if he'd fallen
asleep in his chair.

"Dad, Dad, wake up," I said. I flew into action asking for
Macy's phone.

I called 911 just to be sure. The lady asked if I knew CPR, and I assured her I did.

"Macy come help me move him," I called. She helped me and soon I discovered.

The rigor mortis had kicked in, "I can't do CPR," I exclaimed. "Why not?" the lady asked me.

With a shaky voice, and shaking my head in disbelief, "He's been gone a long time." I stated.

The lady asked me to go outside and wait for the cops to come.

I called my husband, my mom, my siblings, my aunts, my uncles, and my Dad's closest friends.

I answered questions, I insisted that my siblings come to stay with me.

For weeks I couldn't close my eyes without seeing my dead Dad lying there on the floor in the shape of a chair.

12. Yellow

Sunshine, Sunflowers, and Dandelions are warm and bright they bring joyous feelings upon sight.

Basking in the warmth of the sunshine is the perfect treat. Laying on the beach, a trampoline, or even the grass, listening to your own heartbeat.

Petals soft and bright sunflowers always fight. They reach for the sun and lean on each other without wanting to bite.

Dandelions are pretty from afar they litter the grass like they are stars. Considered a weed, they are frowned upon, but they are underestimated and can be fun. You can make bracelets, crayons, food, and wine.

Joyful is the color yellow, once seen it's like a bellow. I am bright, I am warm, I am a happy fellow. Even a bee seems to say, "Look at me, I'm a yellow little bee." Yellow is the way to be.

13. Hurt

It hurts to breathe, it hurts to think, it hurts to be in this
moment.

I see both sides and they all affect me.

This year has been full of learning experiences and
challenges galore. When I voice that I'm overwhelmed
and drowning-that I can't seem to get air, I'm told it's not
as bad as the last years.

I'm not complaining I explain hoping that they realize
I'm not. I LOVE what I do and I just am overwhelmed.
I've never done this before and I'm new...is it so bad that
I don't know what to do? I'm at a loss and grasping for
help, wanting any ideas or ways to cope with stress and
problems that I've never dealt with before.

You're doing great! You're so capable! Thank you so
much! I definitely need the reassurance! However, that's
not why I'm trying to explain what I'm feeling, I

genuinely feel like I'm barely swimming. I'm tired, exhausted, and have a new stressor.

I can handle things, I can do hard things, and I am capable....is that fair though? Is that how things should be? That I work my ass off and do the job of two or three?

I am human...I can't do everything...lately, I'm really dragging. I paste a smile on my face and do my best to act with grace. I don't want to be on the receiving end of someone's distaste.

14. Birthday

You were content to take your sweet time
coming to me baby of mine.
You made me wait seven days overdue
you waited to make your debut.
When you were coming, I was so scared
there was no way I was prepared.
I was convinced I was feeling things and
waited thirteen hours before the internal clock finally
rings.
I went to the hospital full of dread
worried that they would turn me back home with my
face bright red.
The nurses informed me that you'd definitely be coming
today,
"You are at a 7," they said, "Hooray!".
After twenty-three and a half hours, you made your
appearance.
I cried in relief and joy and the nurses commented on my
perseverance.
You had black hair and a cute cleft chin.

I instantly loved you and vowed to love you through thick and thin.

15. Miscarriage

I started feeling sick and couldn't figure out why
When it dawned on me I started to cry.
I can't be pregnant, no please no I think
I run and empty my stomach into the sink.
I buy a pregnancy test and now I'm sure
I'm definitely pregnant, this will be a detour.
I'm in a bad place, I can't do this again.
I let him know and he shrinks in disdain.
Soon he has come to terms with it
And I am wondering if I should admit,
That I am not happy, I don't think I can do this
This life of mine is not pure bliss.
A couple of weeks later I feel pain,
I go into the bathroom and find a blood stain.
Dread creeps and my stomach starts to sink
As the hours drag on it becomes clear that in a blink
I've lost my baby. I cry I rage and hate this situation.
Did me having second thoughts create this aberration?
Did I inadvertently kill it? My sweet little baby that
Was just the size of a fifty-cent piece lying on the mat?

I wanted my baby, I just was scared, God knows that
right?
He won't punish me for being so full of fright?
I didn't want to lose my baby, I hope they know
That even though I couldn't admit it then, I loved their
glow.
I feel so guilty when I think of losing them.
I hope in the afterlife they won't condem.
The young mother who tried to be happy and come to
terms
With the pregnancy only to lose their baby and long to
hold them in her arms.

16. Second Born

My pregnancy with you was hard but it wasn't your
fault you see,
I had a bad relationship with your father and was
accused of being lazy.

You were due October 27th and once that day came and
went
I was determined that you wouldn't be born on
Halloween, so I spent
All day long in pain.

There was an awful pressure on my stomach and off to
the doctor I went. Only to be told I was making it up and
to quit my lament.

Three different times I drove to Delta, I knew you
weren't okay
But no one would check, they said that I needed to just
go away.

By some miracle I got your donor to listen and he took
me to the hospital. The doctors there were so shocked at
my previous rebuttal.

Your baby is stuck in the birthing canal, your doctor is
nuts
Why didn't he catch that? I can't believe he turned you
away, what guts.

They placed an epidural in and half my body went numb
and yet
You still refused to come.
Finally, the next day in the early morning light you made
your appearance and I knew you were just right.

Long, thick, black hair you sported, your cleft chin
reminding me of your sisters. I love you so much, your
my girl I said in hushed whispers.

For weeks, I was punished and unable to hold you other
than to feed and clothe. "No bonding, she's mine." He
would scold.

Finally, he went back to work and I reveled in building
our relationship because you were also my girl and he
was a jerk.

17. Plucked from Pernicious Performances

One day I woke up and just knew deep in my gut
That I was pregnant and thought "What the fuck?".
How did I let this happen? How am I going to be
A single mother and keep my kids from famine?
Eventually, I decided that you were being sent to me
To teach me to stand up for us and not to plea.
It was your sister's first day of Headstart and I knew
You were coming, contractions had been going for a few.
Bound and determined to see her through, I took
care of your other sister as the school day flew.
I got your sisters down for a nap and the next thing I
knew
There was pressure like never before.
I called Grandma and boy she swore.
She came and picked me and your sisters up. She flew to
the hospital, her foot on the gas pedal, and screeched
with a bump.
I walked into the hospital and exclaimed my baby boy is
coming.

The nurses replied there was no rush, and led me to the
room humming.
When she checked me she screamed, "Get the doctor in
here, NOW!"
Everything was chaotic and frantic as they ran around
yelling "WOW".
Exactly ten minutes on the dot after entering the hospital
You arrived making your appearance and man were you
little.
Blondish red hair and a cute nose, you panicked me
when you didn't make a noise.
You were so quiet you seemed like one of the girl's toys.
Your sisters and I instantly loved you and knew you
were meant to be the perfect fit for our family.

18. Ragin Kajun and Ryker Rayne

I was quite pregnant with twins and I was sure
I was going to blow out my leg with my round ligament
so sore.

I prayed that you two boys would be healthy and ready
to come
When I went to the doctor for your monthly check-up.

I was quite surprised when the doctor said baby A had
something to overcome. His umbilical cord was clamped
shut, what a hiccup.

They hustled and induced me right then and there
and I called your dad and gave him quite the scare.

Six hours later I felt pain and sure enough, the nurse
exclaimed.
The babies were coming and we rushed to the O.R.
unashamed.

I had been sick with a cold and I started to cough
And a strange whooshing sensation that was really
rough.

I felt a slickness going down my body, a thump sounded
And I looked at Russell and swore my heart pounded.

The doctor turned as my baby A bungee-ed off his cord
Straight into the garbage can and caused discord.

Once we were sure he was okay, we focused on baby B
next.
The force of Baby A's ejection, caused Baby B to be
perplexed.

He had flipped into the breech position
and the doctor wanted to perform a c-section but I
wouldn't listen.

The doctor said wait a minute and as the contraction
began
She reached up and grabbed baby B's little feet, man I
was not a fan.

Baby B was ripped from me and in the commotion
I learned that he wasn't breathing because of the doctors

motions.

Dad went with Baby B to the ICU and Baby A stayed
with Mom.
After four long hours Baby B was cleared and everyone
was calm.

Baby A was named Kajun and earned the nickname
Ragin from the way he entered the world.

Baby B was named Ryker and his middle name is Rayne
like the world has been cleaned again.

19. Capricious

Calm and caring and then bam
Arragance and anger. Then you are
Peaceful and preening. In a blink your
Raging and revolting. What did I do?
Intensely Interrrogating. I wonder where the
Cute and Cuddly guy went that was there just minutes
before.
I Just can't keep up
Open up and talk to me
Unsteady feelings on the rise
Secretly hoping the positive vibe stays.

20. Loquacious

Lately I find myself
Opening up to
Quiet
Unsuspecting
Adults.
Causing laughter as
I tend to
Overshare embarrassing
Unfolding
Stories that they don't need to hear.

21. Kakorrhaphiophobia

Kindness isn't something that is always
Apparent. Sometimes when someone is
Kind, we wonder why. All we see is
Our faults and our failures.
Realizing that we are subject to
Rejection makes it harder for us to
Jump toward our goals.
Although we shouldn't
Place other people's opinions
High on our lists for ourselves,
It's hard not to worry about feeling
Ostrisized when we struggle to
Perform the way others expect.
How do we stop
Ourselves from feeling
Badly about how
Insecure we are when
Another expresses distaste?